AF598569

Cristiano RONALDO

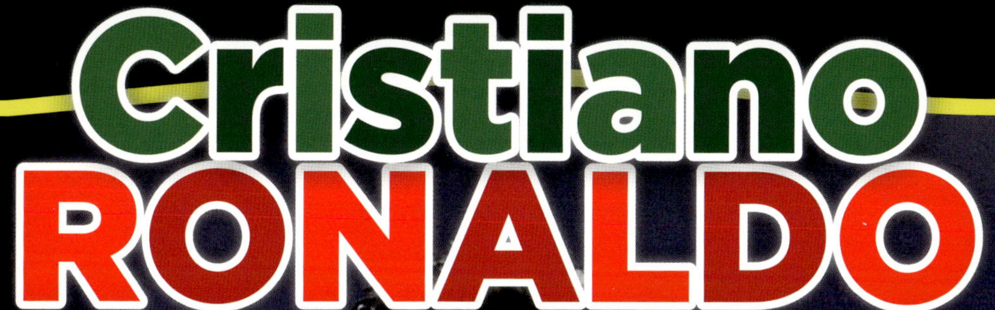

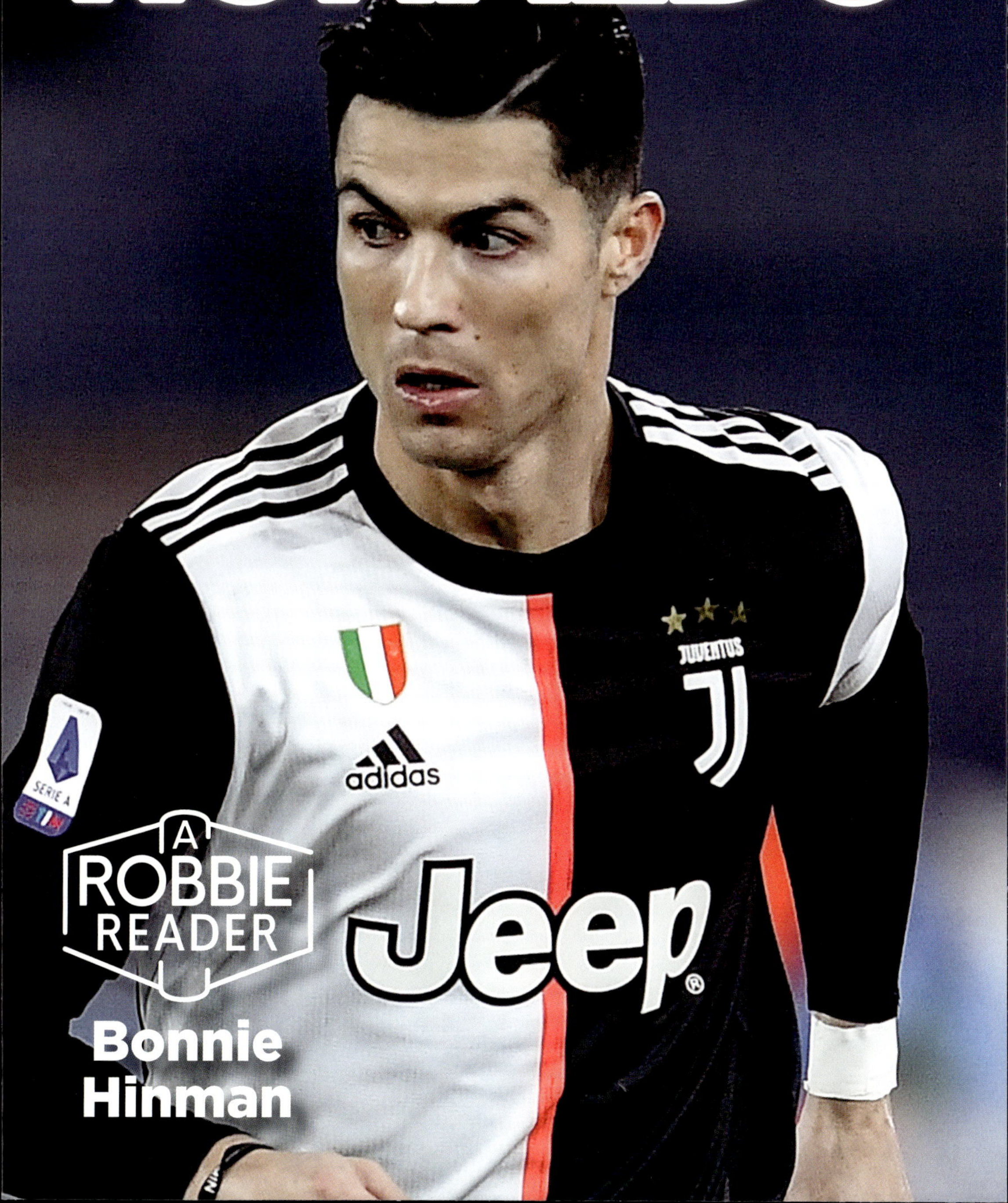

A ROBBIE READER

Bonnie Hinman

2001 SW 31st Avenue
Hallandale, FL 33009

www.mitchelllane.com

First Edition, 2021.
Author: Bonnie Hinman
Designer: Ed Morgan
Editor: Morgan Brody

Series: Robbie Reader
Title: Cristiano Ronaldo / by Bonnie Hinman

Hallandale, FL : Mitchell Lane Publishers, [2021]

Library bound ISBN: 978-1-58415-850-9
eBook ISBN: 978-1-58415-997-1

Little Mitchie is an imprint of Mitchell Lane Publishers.

PHOTO CREDITS: Design Elements, freepik.com, Cover: MASSIMO PINCA/REUTERS/Newscom, p. 5 Giuseppe Maffia/ZUMA Press/Newscom, p. 7 RM3/Rui M Leal / WENN/Newscom, p. 9 DARREN STAPLES/REUTERS/Newscom, p. 10 IAN HODGSON/REUTERS/Newscom, p. 13 Pics United/Icon SMI 792/Pics United/Icon SMI/Newscom, p. 14 Bob Van Der Cruijsem/Pics United/Icon SMI 452, p. 17 JUAN MEDINA/REUTERS/Newscom, pp. 18-19 Alfredo Sanchez/Actionplus/Newscom, p. 21 Fei Maohua Xinhua News Agency/Newscom, p. 23 MAX ROSSI/REUTERS/Newscom, p. 25 JAS LEHAL/REUTERS/Newscom, p. 27 Associated Press

Contents

Words in **bold** can be found in the Glossary.

CHAPTER **ONE**

A YOUNG Soccer STAR

Cristiano Ronaldo started playing for a youth soccer team when he was seven. He scored many goals. His dad took him to the games and cheered for him. However, his mother and sisters did not come to his games. They were polite about his success but not excited.

Before each match started, Cristiano looked up in the stands. He hoped to see his family watching him. But only his father was there to watch Cristiano play. Then one day when he looked up into the stands, he was surprised to see his mother and sisters.

Many years later Ronaldo wrote, “I felt so good in that moment. It meant a lot to me. It was like something switched inside of me. I was really proud.” In those days his family did not have much money. Ronaldo didn’t care about money. He cared about feeling good. “On that day,” Ronaldo wrote, “this feeling, it was very strong. I felt protected and loved.”

Ronaldo controls the ball while looking for an opening to shoot.

CHAPTER **ONE**

Cristiano Ronaldo dos Santos Aveiro was born on the island of Madeira, Portugal, on February 5, 1985. He is the fourth and youngest child of Maria Dolores Spinola dos Santos da Aveiro, a cook, and José Dinis Aveiro, a gardener and a part-time **kit man**. He had an older brother Hugo and two older sisters, Elma and Liliana Catia.

By the time Ronaldo was ten, he was well-known on Madeira as a soccer star. His godfather, Fernao Sousa, told British reporters, "All he wanted to do as a boy was play football (soccer)." Sousa said that Cristiano would escape out his bedroom window to play soccer leaving his homework unfinished.

Those good days with his family were cut short. Ronaldo moved away to attend a soccer **academy**. He was only eleven years old when he left his family.

Ronaldo is a family man. Here he lines up with his family. From the left, brother Hugo, sister Elma, sister Liliana, Cristiano, his mother Dolores, and his brother-in-law Edgar. This photo was taken in Portugal in 2006 after Ronaldo's father had died in 2005.

CHAPTER **TWO**

Sporting **CP** Youth Academy

Scouts for Sporting CP heard about Ronaldo's soccer skills. Located in Lisbon, Sporting CP was one of the top teams in Portugal. They asked Ronaldo to move to Lisbon to live at their youth academy. Youth academies combine school with learning soccer skills.

Ronaldo's parents let him go even though he was only eleven years old. Ronaldo knew it was his big chance. It was still a hard choice. He later said, "I cried almost every day. I didn't know anybody, and it was extremely lonely."

"Football kept me going," Ronaldo said. He made a decision then. "I was going to stop playing like a kid. I was going to stop acting like a kid. I was going to train like I could be the best in the world."

Cristiano in the early days of his soccer career.

Nineteen-year-old Ronaldo training with Manchester United in March 2004.

Sporting CP Youth Academy

Ronaldo moved through the different levels playing for the academy teams. He stopped going to school when he was fourteen. He wanted to focus all his efforts on playing soccer.

At age fifteen Ronaldo had surgery to correct a heart problem. It was serious and could have ended his soccer career. **Laser surgery** corrected the **defect**. He was back at practice in a few days.

When Ronaldo was seventeen, he began his **professional** career for Sporting CP of Lisbon. At eighteen, he was signed by England's Manchester United club. Manchester was one of the best teams in Europe. They paid Sporting CP 12.24 million **pounds** to transfer Ronaldo to Manchester.

Ronaldo made his first appearance for Manchester as a substitute on August 16, 2003. On November 3, 2003, he made his first goal for Manchester. He improved with each game. Ronaldo helped his team win **tournaments** including the Premier League Championship. Ronaldo won the Ballon d'Or award in 2008. This award was presented each year to the best soccer player in Europe.

CHAPTER **THREE**

Portuguese National Team

Ronaldo played for the Portuguese national team beginning in 2003. National soccer teams have players born in their country. Team members play for their regular team like Manchester United or Real Madrid. They also play for their national team if asked. Most national team games and practices happen during the regular season. Players miss some of their club's games to be on their national team.

Ronaldo played in his first World Cup tournament in 2006. World Cup tournaments are held every four years in different countries. National teams compete to attend the World Cup. The 2006 World Cup was held in Germany. Ronaldo played well in his first World Cup appearance.

Ronaldo helps Portugal defeat Angola in a first round match during the 2006 FIFA World Cup in Cologne, Germany.

CHAPTER **THREE**

Ronaldo draws the referee's attention to fellow Portuguese player, Ricardo Carvalho, who was injured by English player Wayne Rooney. Rooney and Ronaldo were teammates on their regular Manchester United team.

However, English fans turned against him when a fellow Manchester United player was **penalized**. Wayne Rooney played for the English national team. During the quarterfinal match with Portugal, Rooney was sent off the field for stomping on a Portuguese player. English fans blamed Ronaldo for the penalty. They shouted at him each time he appeared. The shouting continued for a time after the teammates came home to play for Manchester.

Ronaldo's personal life had some ups and downs while he played for Manchester. His father died in 2005. Jose was only 52 years old. He died of a drinking-related liver problem. In 2007 Ronaldo's mother had breast cancer. Maria was treated and recovered.

Ronaldo gave large amounts of money to different charities. In 2004 he raised $6 million for victims of the Indian Ocean earthquake and **tsunami**. In 2009 Ronaldo donated over $124,000 to build a cancer center. The money went to the Madeira hospital that treated his mother's breast cancer.

In 2010 Ronaldo became a father. His son Cristiano Jr. was born June 17, 2010. This was an important day for the family-loving Ronaldo.

CHAPTER **FOUR**

Real MADRID

Each year Ronaldo scored more goals for Manchester United. In the 2007–2008 season he scored 42 goals. He also led the team to win first place in both the Champions League and the Premier League tournaments.

Real Madrid tried to get Ronaldo to move to their club after that big year. Ronaldo decided to stay with Manchester United for one more season. United won their third straight league title. After the 2008–2009 season Ronaldo moved to Real Madrid. That team paid a $130 million transfer price to Manchester United. Ronaldo signed a six-year contract with his new club.

Ronaldo was presented to Real Madrid fans on July 6, 2009, as the newest player to join the team. His presentation and welcome drew at least 80,000 fans to the stadium in Madrid.

bwin

Ronaldo scored 33 goals in 35 appearances during his first season with Real Madrid in 2009–2010. He scored four goals in a single game during the 2010–2011 season. This was a career first for him. The goals kept piling up as he scored 60 in the 2011–2012 season. That same season he led his team to the La Liga division championship. La Liga is the men's top professional football division of the Spanish football league system.

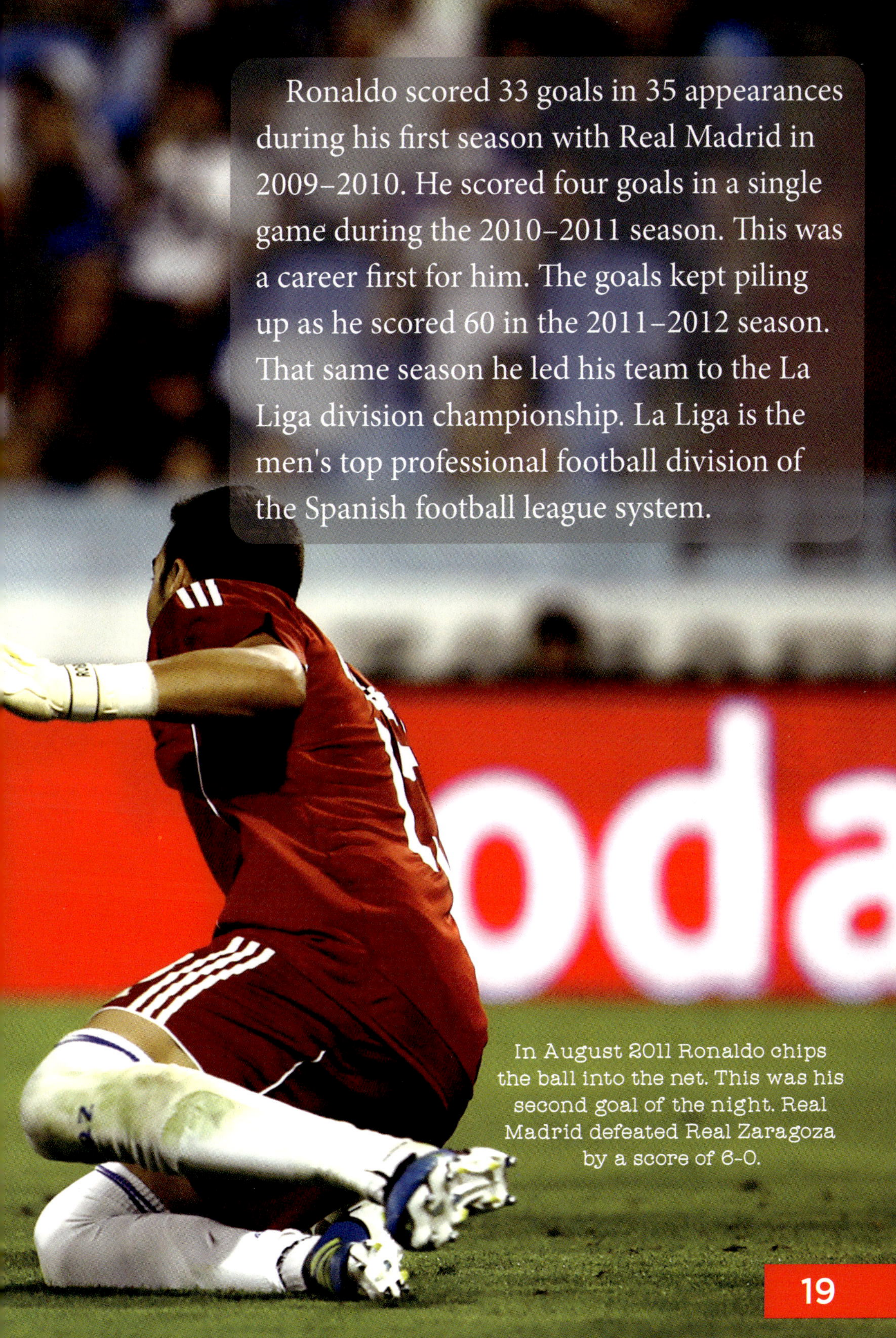

In August 2011 Ronaldo chips the ball into the net. This was his second goal of the night. Real Madrid defeated Real Zaragoza by a score of 6-0.

CHAPTER **FOUR**

Ronaldo continued to give large amounts of money to charities. In 2012 he helped pay for cancer treatment for a nine-year-old Spanish boy. In 2015 he donated over $6 million to help victims of an earthquake in Nepal. In 2016 he donated his Champions League bonus to various charities.

International play saw Ronaldo competing in the World Cup in 2010, 2014, and 2018. Unlike Ronaldo's performance in the 2006 World Cup, his next two World Cup appearances were not great. He had trouble with injuries and scored few goals. His fourth World Cup in 2018 went better. Real Madrid came into the tournament as European champions. However, that was it for him and soon for Real Madrid. They lost to Uruguay and left the tournament.

Ronaldo argues with a referee during a 2018 World Cup game pitting Portugal against Uruguay. Portugal lost that game and was eliminated from the tournament.

7
REFEREE
FIFA
2018

CHAPTER **FIVE**

Juventus

Ronaldo's contract with Real Madrid ended after the 2017–2018 season. He signed with Juventus, an Italian team, in July 2018. He took a pay cut by signing for $64 million per year. Juventus paid a $140 million **transfer** fee to Real Madrid. Ronaldo also asked for contributions to his youth clubs.

Real Madrid player Ronaldo works at keeping the ball away from Juventus player Rodrigo Bentancur in April 2018. Shortly after this game Ronaldo transferred from Real Madrid to the Juventus team.

He first became a father to a son, Cristiano Jr., born on June 17, 2010. Ronaldo then became a father to twins, daughter Eva Maria and son Mateo born on June 8, 2017 via **surrogacy**. Daughter Alana Martina arrived in November 2017. Her mom is Ronaldo's girlfriend Georgina Rodriguez. Legal problems gave Ronaldo some worries in 2017. He was charged with tax evasion in Spain. In June 2018 he agreed to pay a fine of $21.7 million. He also received a two-year **suspended** jail sentence.

CHAPTER **FIVE**

Ronaldo is one of the kings of social media. By the end of 2018, Ronaldo had 340 million followers on Facebook, Instagram, and Twitter. Advertisers pay to have their ads appear on his social media posts. He made close to $400,000 on each of his **sponsored** posts on Instagram in 2018. Ronaldo spends much of his money **investing** in his own businesses. He owns underwear, footwear, blanket, and fragrance businesses.

Ronaldo speaks at the launch of a new Nike soccer boot on February 28, 2010, in London. His large social media following makes him a popular choice to advertise new products.

In Ronaldo's first season with Juventus, he scored 28 goals in 43 appearances. Juventus won the Serie A division title for the season. Ronaldo was voted best player of the 2018–2019 Serie A. He also led his Portuguese national team to their first-ever UEFA Nations League title.

While visiting family in Madeira in June 2019, Ronaldo spoke to reporters. Ronaldo said of the new season to come, "I'm always ready. I want to have a good season, that's always my goal. Year after year I want to do the best I can and win titles."

Being ready and doing his best may lead Cristiano to fulfill his dream of being the best soccer player in the world. His drive and ambition make that honor within reach.

Timeline

1985 Cristiano Ronaldo is born on February 5 on Madeira Island in Portugal.

1992 Begins playing soccer for a local youth team.

1996 Moves to Lisbon to attend the Sporting CP Youth Academy.

2000 Has laser heart surgery to correct defect.

2002 Plays for Sporting CP professional club.

2003 Joins Manchester United soccer club; plays for Portuguese national team.

2006 Plays in first World Cup in Germany.

2008 Wins the Ballon d'Or award as the best soccer player in Europe.

2009 Moves to Real Madrid soccer club.

2012 Leads Real Madrid to La Liga division championship.

2016 Donates Champions League bonus to charities.

2017 Charged with tax evasion in Spain; later pays fine.

2018 Moves to Juventus soccer club in Italy.

2019 Voted best player of the 2018–2019 Serie A division.

Find Out More

Official website for Juventus Football Club
https://www.juventus.com/en/

Official website for the Union of European Football Associations
https://www.uefa.com

Official website for World Cup Qatar 2022
https://www.fifa.com/worldcup/qatar2022/

Works Consulted

Abdulazeez, Amir. "The Greatest Player? Messi vs. Ronaldo." *Modern Trader*. January 2018. MasterFILE Premier. Accession Number 127422680

Biography.com Editors. "Cristiano Ronaldo." Biography.com. June 29, 2019. https:www.biography.com/athlete/cristiano-ronaldo

"Cristiano Ronaldo, Forward." *Juventus*. https://www.juventus.com/en/teams/first-team/forwards/cristiano-ronaldo/index.php

"Cristiano Ronaldo Biography Facts." Sportytell.com. April 30, 2019. https://sportytell.com/football/cristiano-ronaldo-biography-facts-childhood-personal-life/

"Cristiano Ronaldo Funds Cancer Treatment for 9-Year-Old boy." https://as.com/diarioas/2012/06/19/english/1340056811_850210.html

Critchley, Mark. "Cristiano Ronaldo: Real Madrid Forward Donates (Euros Symbol)600,000 Champions League Win Bonus to Charity." *Independent*. June 3, 2016. https://www.independent.co.uk/sport/football/european/cristiano-ronaldo-real-madrid-forward-donates-600000-champions-league-final-bonus-to-charity-a7063036.html

Davies, Hunter. "The Fan." *New Statesman*. January 10, 2014. MasterFILE Premier. Accession Number 93602634

Forbes Lists. "#2 Cristiano Ronaldo: 2019 The World's Highest-Paid Athletes Earnings." *Forbes*. June 10, 2019. https://www.forbes.com/profile/cristiano-ronaldo/#29d849d8565d

Geeter, Darren. "The Business of Being Cristiano Ronaldo." CNBC. June 15, 2018. https://www.cnbc.com/2018/06/15/cristiano-ronaldo-world-cup-football-soccer-michael-jordan-real-madrid.html

Grabianowski, Ed. "How Soccer Works: Soccer Leagues and Championship Cups." How Stuff Works, https://entertainment.howstuffworks.com/soccer3.htm

Works Consulted *continued*

Harigovind. "Cristiano Ronaldo Reveals His Targets With Juventus in the 2019-20 Season." Fox Sports Asia. July 8, 2019. https://www.foxsportasia.com/football/serie-a/1135848/Cristiano-ronaldo-reveals-targets-juventus-2019-20-season/

Kelly, Ryan. "Cristiano Ronaldo's History at the World Cup: 2006 Debut, 2014 Heartache & Record-Breaking 2018." Goal.com. July 2, 2018. https://www.goal.com/en-us/news/cristiano-ronaldos-history-at-the-world-cup-2006-debut-2014/3gago097ess01szjb0ve7nhu9

Lewis, Tim. "He's Got the World At His Feet." *The Guardian*. June 7, 2008. https://www.theguardian.com/football/2008/jun/08/manchesterunited.portugal

Marcotti, Gabriele. "Cristiano Ronaldo." *Sports Illustrated*: XI for '11. MasterFILE Premier, Accession Number 61283179

Menezes, Jack de. "Cristiano Ronaldo 'Agrees' Two Year Suspended Jail Sentence and (Euros Symbol)18.8m Fine Over Tax Evasion Case." *Independent*. June 15, 2018. https://www.independent.co.uk/sport/football/world-cup/cristiano-ronaldo-jail-sentence-two-years-suspended-tax-evasion-case-fine-how-much-world-cup-2018-a8400631.html

"Real Madrid's All-Time Leading Goalscorer." *Real Madrid CF*. https://www.realmadrid.com/en/about-real-madrid/history/football-legends/cristiano-ronaldo-dos-santos-aveiro

Roco, Alvaro. "Cristiano Ronaldo: The Social Media King." *Marca*, October 20, 2018. https://www.marca.com/en/football/international-football/2018/10/20/5bca53b7e2704e11378b463d.html

Ronaldo, Cristiano. "Cristiano Ronaldo's Farewell Letter." *Real Madrid* CF, October 7, 2018. https://www.realmadrid.com/en/news/2018/07/Cristiano-ronaldos-farewell-letter

Ronaldo, Cristiano. "Madrid: My Story." *The Players Tribune*. October 3, 2017. https://www.theplayerstribune.com/en-us/articles/cristiano-ronaldo-madrid-english

"Ronaldo First to Win Five Champions League Titles." *UEFA*. May 26, 2018. https://www.uefa.com/uefachampionsleague/news/newsid=2475340.html

Glossary

academy
A school that offers special instruction in a field

defect
Lack of something necessary to be normal

evasion
Avoiding of a duty or requirement

international
Between or among nations

investing
To use money to earn more money

kit man
Equipment manager for the football (soccer) association

laser surgery
A type of surgery that uses special light beams instead of instruments

penalized
To give a team or player a disadvantage because of poor conduct

pounds
A unit of money used in England

professional
Earning one's living by playing a sport

sponsored
To pay to have a person or company's name mentioned

surrogate
A woman who becomes pregnant and has a child for someone else

suspended
To stop doing something temporarily as a punishment

transfer
To move (a player) to another team in exchange for money

tournaments
Sports competitions, contests or matches

tsunami
A huge wave caused by an earthquake under an ocean

Index

About the **Author**

Bonnie Hinman has written more than 60 books for young people about many subjects. Soccer is an exciting game and it was fun to write about the determined and talented Cristiano Ronaldo. Hinman lives in Southwest Missouri with her husband and near her children and five grandchildren.